ANNUALS
AND BEDDING PLANTS

PAT WEAVER

HarperCollins*Publishers*

Products mentioned in this book

Benlate* + 'Activex'	contains	benomyl
'Picket'	contains	permethrin
ICI Slug Pellets	contains	metaldehyde
'Sybol'	contains	pirimiphos-methyl

Products marked thus '*Sybol*' are trade marks of Imperial Chemical Industries plc
'Benlate' is a registered trade mark of Du Pont's
Read the label before you buy; use pesticides safely

Editors Maggie Daykin, Susanne Mitchell
Designer Chris Walker
Production Controller Craig Chubb
Picture research Moira McIlroy

First published 1989 by
HarperCollins Publishers

This edition published 1992

© Marshall Cavendish Limited 1989, 1992

A CIP catalogue record for this book is available from the British Library.

Photoset by Litho Link Ltd., Welshpool, Powys, Wales
Printed and bound in Hong Kong by Dai Nippon Printing Company

Front cover: Summer bedding plants by The Harry Smith Horticultural
Collection
Back cover: Cottage Garden by Michael Warren

CONTENTS

INTRODUCTION

The idea of massing plants to heighten the effect of flower form and colour has been with us since late Victorian times. Fashions in planting may change but the concept remains the same. The setting is an open bed, oval, square or crescent shaped, and the general effect is a carpet of living colour. Plants should be at their peak of blooming and capable of surviving all weathers. They must also be of uniform size, relatively easy to maintain and pest free.

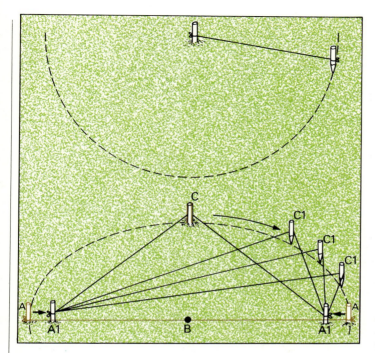

right angles to this, drive in a stake C. Mark on a piece of cord the exact length of the bed, from stake to stake, leaving extra cord beyond each mark.

Then, pull out each stake A and tie each to the cord at the marked spot. Loop the middle of the cord around C. Get help, pull the cord taut and drive in the two stakes again along the long axis A1.

Loosen the stake C, and slide it along the length of the cord, marking the turf as you go, C1. This will indicate half the oval. Repeat on the other side.

TOP
To make a circular bed, decide its location and size, then drive in a stake at the centre. Attach a piece of cord equal in length to half the required diameter. At the other end fix a pointed stick and use this to score a circle round the centrally placed stake.

BOTTOM
To make an oval bed, drive in two stakes, one at each end of its long axis A. Drive in another stake halfway in between – B. At

Victorian taste in flowers was conditioned by the gentry who had vast complexes of heated greenhouses. Large quantities of pelargoniums, annuals and sub-tropical shrubs such as eucalyptus, cordylines and yuccas were grown and maintained in this heated atmosphere until the time came to plant them out. Designs based on the intricate patterns of Persian carpets were popular and a challenge to ambitious gardeners.

Modern bedding
Now, tastes have changed and mass bedding has adapted itself to the smaller, modern garden. But the creation of a long lasting display is still a worthwhile gardening occupation if not overdone – and restricted to one part of the garden. There is also a challenge in selecting plants that will be complementary in terms of size and colour. A scheme based on not more than three colours works very well.

Repeated use of the same beds for a long continuous display of flowers will, of course, quickly exhaust soil nutrients. The answer is to feed and cultivate the ground with a general fertilizer such as growmore before plants are put out. This is essential if the bed used for spring bedding has to follow on immediately with a compact summer display as well.

Wallflowers, forget-me-nots and tulips lend themselves well to mass springtime bedding. All can be bought in the autumn and planted where they are to bloom. Spring-flowering pansies are long lasting and delicate; try the F_1 form 'Imperial Orange Prince' or, if you like blue, 'Azure Blue'. *Bellis perennis* in the Monstrosa forms makes a pretty edging. *Kaufmanniana* and *greigii* tulips produce ground-hugging foliage and bloom at a height of around 25cm (10in).

Catalogues offer a bewildering range of half-hardy annuals, so reduce your options by deciding your colour scheme before trying to select the plants. The challenge then lies in devising combinations of plants that are of uniform size. Ultimate spread must also be taken into account, to prevent over-crowding or leaving bare ground.

Focal points A dot plant is a dramatically attractive plant with large decorative leaves (and sometimes flowers that are insignificant compared with the foliage) used as a central or focal point among massed bedding. To fill this very important role, look out for plants such as the castor oil plant, *Ricinus communis,* with its plum coloured leaves, or burning bush, *Kochia scoparia* which masquerades as a fluffy conifer then, come September, takes on a red hue. *Cineraria maritima* is exceptionally good with cerise petunias and will often winter outdoors. The choice is much wider than this, of course, but will depend on the plants selected for your basic scheme.

ABOVE The chocolate-striped grey-green, lanceolate leaves of *Tulipa greigii* provide the perfect foil for forget-me-nots.

RIGHT *Kochia scoparia trichophila* makes a particularly striking focal point as it takes on its reddish autumn hues.

IMPORTANCE OF COLOUR

Of all plant characteristics, flower colour has the most immediate impact. Success in combining colours does not always come easily and, indeed, often occurs accidentally. Sometimes this teaches a most useful lesson in colour-gardening and sparks off new, bold ideas. Clearly, though, the best results are achieved when deliberate plantings are made with an eye to the ultimate mass colour-effect.

A successful mass colour effect can best be achieved with tones of just two or three colours as in this planting of echeverias, alyssum, petunias and tagetes.

It should be said however, that any elaborate mass or carpet-planting based on flowers grown from seed, is necessarily restricted to the spring and summer seasons. Flowers from seed, even those that like shade, need some sunlight too. They also need some warm weather for germinating, growing and blooming.

White is perfect for bringing a sense of light into dark corners of the garden, and it can be introduced in various ways. In a shady border, place the perennial white *Viola cornuta* where it can weave its white flowers up and through ferns, ajugas and the pale blue spikes of nepeta.

The annual *Nicotiana sylvestris*, a tall 2m (6ft) plant, produces its candelabras of white trumpet-flowers

the first summer. Site it to lighten a dark fence or shady wall. Coming as it does bountifully from seed, this attractive half-hardy annual should be grown more often.

Perennial white arabis and cerastium on the rock-garden are nice foils and set off alpine phlox to perfection. *Bellis perennis* 'White Carpet' should always be planted alongside the 'Rose' and 'Red Carpet' forms of this lovely and very popular May-flowering biennial.

Silver foliage plants have the same 'light' characteristic as white ones but with the most pleasant addition of furry and velvet-textured foliage. Their use is endless. For example, lamb's ears (*Stachys lanata*) planted at the front of a border will set off

8

the crimson flower-heads of September sedums in bloom at the same time. Also, the purple flowers of *S. lanata* provide a nice contrast to its silvery foliage.

Try teaming it with the salmon-flowered perennial *Phlox* 'Windsor', or the deep gold of the annual *Rudbeckia* 'Marmalade'. The silver cinerarias such as 'Cirrhus' or 'Silver Dust' are fast growing perennials that make enough growth in their first year to be useful as dot-plantings among annuals or perhaps to enliven the green foliage of a mixed long border.

You will find that all silvers contrast with and enhance cerise, pink and lemon petunias, also a warm, sunshine combination of gold and orange French and African marigolds.

Silver plants generally bloom in late summer. The flowers are usually pale lemon and insignificant compared with the foliage, but nevertheless a nice addition to any planting scheme.

Green flowers are always of interest, because green is normally thought of as a foliage colour. My own favourite will always be the half-hardy annual, *Nicotiana* 'Lime Green'. For the best colour-effect, plant very closely since the plant's habit is vertical rather than bushy.

Lime-green is a good colour to complement and cool down the hot look of red cosmos 'Diablo' or the red nasturtium 'Empress of India'. It also associates well with mauve and pink michaelmas daisies as well as callistephus (mixed half-hardy asters).

Moluccella laevis is a green 'curiosity' that always attracts attention. Its bell-like flower-heads have earned it the popular name of bells of Ireland.

ABOVE Grey-green *Helichrysum petiolatum* here offsets the soft pink of *Pelargonium* 'Hollywood Star'. A nice choice for patio pots, too.

RIGHT *Moluccella leavis* is a very popular and distinctive green-flowered plant.

Nemophila insignis, a very attractive spreading plant; its blue flowers with white centres are complemented by delightful feathery foliage.

Blue is the colour of misty distances and, logically, it should be used as a background foil for the hotter orange and red shades. On a small scale, try *Nigella damascena* 'Gertrude Jekyll', for its spiky, blue flowers that bloom at about 23cm (9in). This plant has an extended lease of life, as balloon-shaped seed pods follow on. *Nemophila insignis* (baby blue eyes) has a low, spreading habit that suggests a generous planting of this lovely hardy annual along a sunny path.

Also, there is a wide range of sky-blue violas and pansies, notably 'Ullswater' (deep blue), 'Blue Heaven' (mid blue) and 'Azure Blue'. All are hardy perennials, usually grown as half-hardy annuals – reared under glass and put out in May for summer flowering.

Golden-yellow Discounting white, this is the lightest colour in the spectrum. It can be safely said that there are more yellow flowers than any other single colour, which means there is a very wide range of plants to choose from for your colour-scheme.

Mixing colours One colour alone is never visually satisfying; you need some fill-in plantings of at least two or more colours. For instance, a broad display of African marigolds is totally wrong but comes to life if gold, lemon and orange forms of varying heights are used along with complementary plantings of blue and purple flowers. Lobelia comes in both these shades and makes a perfect edging to drifts of French marigolds such as the golden single

'Silvia' – a low one at 20cm (8in) – and the double gold 'Goldfinch'.

Use white nicotiana in close-planted groups to cut up the overpowering effect of massed yellow flowers. *Stachys lanata* and the lovely *Salvia argentea* (a real charmer with velvety ear-like foliage) make a very colourful and balanced scheme using mainly yellow and white. White alyssum, aubrieta and arabis are just three of the long-lasting and obvious choices.

The secret of success is to study (and enjoy) your seed catalogues. Be prepared to experiment with all sorts of plant-material, some from seed, others as established plants already in the garden.

For an easy spring colour-scheme, try wallflowers, perhaps the bright 'Cloth of Gold', as the basis for a flowery corner. Relieve this with blue forget-me-nots, again from seed. Dot-plant with mauve, lily-flowered tulips. Enhance wall-flowers of the variety 'Primrose Bedder' – more sulphur-coloured than gold – by a planting of palest pink, mid-season tulips.

RIGHT Golden yellow spring flowers are a cheering sight at the end of a long winter. The choice of plants in this colour is considerable, but no spring border would be complete without a display of waxen-headed tulips.

RIGHT *Nicotiana affine* 'Dwarf White Bedder', with its dainty clusters of white flowers, is a good companion plant for sunny yellows.

LEFT Brilliant pink *Mesembryanthemum criniflorum* teamed with white *Alyssum maritimum* in a bed of mixed annuals.

BELOW The dramatic spikes of *Cordyline australis* making the desired impact in among the annual bedding.

Pink is always a pretty colour to play with since it graduates from pale fresh tints through rose to deep carmine. Its best colour companions are purple and mauve. See how this works out in a circular bed with *Antirrhinum* 'Lavender Monarch' alternating freely with the rosy alyssum called 'Wonderland' and the bright pink form of *Impatiens* 'Futura'.

As a centrepiece, choose the spectacular *Lavatera trimestris* 'Silver Cup' for its dramatic, rich pink, petunia-like flowers. It blooms at around 1.2m (4ft) and, if well grown, should stand high above the rest of the plants in the bed. Alternatively, use nicotiana in a purple, pink and white mixture.

All the above are half-hardy annuals that can be grown from seed sown in the spring for flowering from May onwards (start them from seed germinated indoors). They will all continue to bloom till the first autumn frosts cut them down.

Red is the most difficult colour to work with since it can 'burn a hole' in any scheme, drawing the eye to it and diminishing the power of all other bright colours. But this hottest colour in the whole spectrum can be charming and exciting if complemented by the right colours. Opt for an uncompromising scarlet, as seen in *Salvia* 'Blaze of Fire', and plan other colours round it.

Above all, avoid using white with red. Usually invaluable in pastel pink and lemon schemes, white always looks uneasy in association with bold, red flowers, whereas mahogany, copper and deep crimson complement hot red to perfection. Bushy *Perilla atropurpurea laciniata* is a half-hardy annual that grows to 60cm (2ft), provides the crimson touch and is suitable as a dot-plant among scarlet flowers.

Amaranthus 'Illumination' is an exotic foliage plant that has purple and crimson in its leaves, and a volcano-red centre. This one needs the full half-hardy treatment, being reared indoors and planted out in the garden at the end of May.

Green provides a cool, natural counterpoint to all red flowers. *Kochia scoparia* (burning bush) has attractive, green, bush-like foliage till September, then takes on an autumnal crimson splendour. Or try *Cordyline australis,* a spiky palm that makes a spectacular dot-plant and will survive the winter in warmer parts of the country. It is best pot-grown so that it can be moved about the garden to wherever it can be seen to best effect. Then, in November, it can be taken into the greenhouse for over-wintering.

Above all, dismiss from your mind the idea that a Persian carpet display of random flowers makes a colourful garden. You would find it restless and hard on the eye. Instead, direct your thoughts to colour schemes using only three or so colours, and you will be immensely satisfied with the result.

ABOVE Pale lemon yellow, deep gold, white and blue scheme for bedding in a small garden.

LEFT A charming, cottage garden effect in which the colourful, flower-packed border is the perfect complement for white painted brick and blackened timbers.

SEED SOWING

The pleasure of growing summer flowering plants from seed cannot be over-rated; the simple activity of producing, or seeming to produce, something from nothing, is unbelievably rewarding. Success lies in understanding that seeds need moisture to germinate, warmth and a rooting medium to start forming their first roots, then light to produce stems and leaves – and in efficiently arranging these practicalities.

Scatter seed lightly over the surface of the chosen medium then cover with a thin layer of the same prepared compost. Water, using a fine rose on the watering can, and cover with a sheet of glass topped by paper to keep out any light until the seeds begin to germinate. Remember to label the box before setting it in a warm, dry place such as a greenhouse or airing cupboard.

Half-hardy annuals such as petunias and lobelia require a longer summer for growth than hardy annuals. Started outdoors, half-hardies would be naturally coming into bloom in early autumn. This is obviously unsatisfactory since these plants are wanted as the mainstay of summer bedding schemes. The answer has always been to grow half-hardy annuals under glass and to accelerate their growth in the warmer temperatures of a greenhouse, in readiness for putting outdoors at the end of May. With due care, they can be in bloom only a few short weeks later.

The first step is to select a suitable medium in which to germinate the seed, such as John Innes No. 1 compost or a soilless compost such as 'Kericompost'. Both are equally good, but the same sort of compost should be used in the seed-boxes when it comes to transplanting.

Seed germinates best in a smooth growing medium, so remove any lumps by running the soil through the fingers, or putting it through a medium sieve. After four weeks your seedlings should be ready for the next stage, 'boxing on'.

Seed is usually started into growth in early March. Where only a small amount of each variety is required, 8cm (3in) pots are quite suitable. Used plastic cups, yoghurt or margarine containers make economical 'pots' suitable for sowing

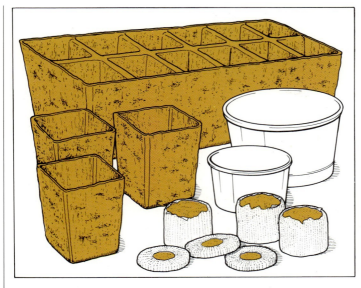

As well as the excellent choice of small pots and cell trays sold commercially, you can improvise by using any small plastic container – such as a yoghurt pot or margarine carton – but pierce the base to provide adequate drainage and make sure that these containers are scrupulously clean before sowing in them.

small quantities of seed. But all pots and boxes must have a drainage hole in the bottom and be thoroughly cleaned before use.

You will also need labels to identify all your sowings. Plastic labels are always satisfactory; write on them with a marker pen containing indelible fade-resistant ink. I find that an ordinary HB pencil also makes a firm, weather-proof record. Labels should also be dated at sowing-time.

Handle opened packets with the greatest care to avoid wasteful spillage; some varieties are very fine and seed is expensive, particularly F_1 hybrid seed specially bred to produce plants of great vigour and with a consistent flowering performance. (When grown from seed, your plants are unlikely to produce seed that comes true).

Compost should be thoroughly moistened several hours before sowing. Allow surplus moisture to drain away until the compost 'balls up' if lightly squeezed in your palm.

This will provide just the right amount of moisture to initiate the germination process.

Large seeds are easy to sow, particularly if they are of a quite different colour from the growing medium. Space them out to allow plenty of growing room. Lightly cover with your chosen compost.

Small seeds such as begonias, calceolarias and impatiens need more care. Empty the contents of the seed packet into a small container and mix in a little dry sand then distribute this over the surface of the compost, or simply press these fine seeds into the compost and do not cover them at all.

Pelleted seeds are individually encased in a white covering of fertilizer that provides the nutrients for germination and rapid growth. It also makes sowing small seeds very much easier and, in my own experience, they can still be viable for sowing in the following year.

Germination Having sown your seed, you must now encourage it to germinate in a warm place. This could be a small plastic propagator with an electric heating element set into the base and a transparent cover to retain the right amount of heat and moisture.

More expensive, but also more efficient, are larger propagators with thermostats to regulate the heat, and sliding panel covers to allow you to adjust the ventilation.

Otherwise, you can simply cover pots with a sheet of glass or a polythene bag (a clean, new one) and put them in your airing cupboard. A small thermometer by the pots will enable you to control temperature by opening or closing the door. I have successfully germinated thousands of half-hardy annuals in this way over the years.

Germination temperatures vary according to the seed being sown, but usually fall within the 18°C to 25°C (65 to 75°F) range. Pelargoniums, in particular, need 25°C (75°F) and must be sown in January if they are to give a full season of flowers. African and French marigolds need 20°C (68 to 70°F) but are usually up within five days.

Large seeds are easily germinated in a plastic sandwich-box. Simply spread dampened paper kitchen-towelling over the bottom and put the seeds on it, pressing them gently into the towelling. Close the lid and put in a warm, dark place as already described.

Some seeds, such as sweet peas, have a thick protective coating which should be carefully nicked to allow moisture to soak into the seed more easily.

If you are germinating seeds in a greenhouse, a maximum-minimum thermometer will tell you how warm or cold the atmosphere was the previous night. This is especially important if you want to sow spring seed during the early months of the year.

Nicotianas will only respond if kept in the light during the germination process. They usually take some time to come anyway.

Large seeds can be germinated on a couple of layers of dampened kitchen towelling laid in the base of a plastic sandwich-box. Gently press the seeds into the surface of the towel, close the lid and place in a suitable spot until they germinate.

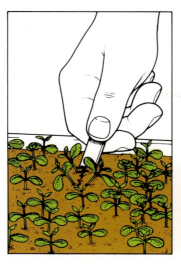

The next stage is to transplant or 'prick off' the small seedlings into a seed tray, filled with potting compost. Or you can transfer stronger plants to single pots. Handle the plants by the leaves only to avoid damaging the stems.

Preventing mould-growth Once your seeds are sown, spray the surface of the compost with a systemic fungicide such as Benlate + 'Activex' to prevent mould-growth. Inspect all your seed-pots and boxes every few days to ensure that all is going well.

When signs of growth appear above the soil, bring that particular container into the half-light. Gradually bring all germinated seedlings showing this top-growth into full light.

Guard against damping off (stems look furry, then the plantlet collapses) by again spraying with a fungicide according to directions.

Growing on As seedlings grow and put forth stems and baby-leaves, grow them on in clean seed-boxes with good drainage and again, using John Innes No. 1 compost or a peat-based compost such as 'Kericompost'.

Ensure that soil is not lumpy, and that the surface has a very fine tilth. Spray your seedlings lightly with lukewarm water, before carefully lifting them with the root intact.

Plant in the soil to the depth of the baby-leaves, so they are flush with the soil. Keep in a warm, light situation, preferably in a greenhouse. Water well and spray with Benlate + 'Activex' fungicide.

During the following weeks continue to keep well watered and after four to six weeks, give a dilute liquid feed such as Liquid Growmore.

Spacing of plants in boxes is critical. My own criterion is 20 to 24 plants per box. This method produces large young plants. None will be in bloom when put out in the garden in late May, but the plants will be bushy and of a good size. There will also be a profusion of flowers in time for my summer flower display.

Some half-hardy annuals do better if each plant is grown on in a separate pot. I have in mind *Amaranthus caudatus*, lavatera and sweet peas. Small, extra deep peat pots are ideal since they enable young plants to be planted direct into the garden without any root disturbance. The pots eventually disintegrate in the open soil and allow the growing roots to spread comfortably.

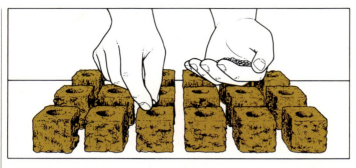

TOP LEFT Small, individual soil blocks allow you to sow seeds separately and later plant them out without disturbing tender young roots.

LEFT Thin out the young seedlings as necessary to ensure healthy, vigorous growth.

RIGHT Mark out annual beds in bays as shown. Sow the seed by scattering, or in drills, then carefully rake over to cover. Finally, label each small plot.

Easy-care seedlings Nowadays, seedsmen offer easy-care alternatives to rearing large quantities of plants from seed. One advertises a consignment of tight-packed seedlings in a plastic box. This is very useful with begonias, impatiens, petunias, primroses and salvias. All produce very tiny seeds that a home-gardener may not have the equipment or patience to nurture.

Seedlings individually grown in compost blocks are also available. Ageratum and summer-flowering begonia hybrids are among the plants sold in this form.

However germinated or grown-on, plant out all half-hardy annuals from the middle of May. Space generously, evaluating the room to be taken up by individual plants. As a rough guide, the length of your trowel is about right for spacing African marigolds, petunias and cosmos, while the length of the blade usually suffices for lobelia, alyssum and plants of similar proportions and habit of growth.

Bought plants From April onwards, garden-centres carry huge stocks of half-hardy annuals, all suitable for summer bedding, outdoor containers and window-boxes. Enjoy looking at what is offered but be wary when buying. Avoid plants that are in full bloom; select those with little or no show of flower colour. Look also for plants sold in plastic 'strips', since these are likely to have been grown from seed undisturbed. All you have to do is break open the 'strip' and carefully ease out the plants.

General care For all half-hardy annuals, water well in as soon as planted and remove all flower-buds for the first two weeks. This will encourage your young plants to bush out more. Watch out for pests, notably thrips on French marigolds in June. Plants infected with them are often partially defoliated, the flower-buds having a stark 'matchstick' look. Plentiful watering, even douching plants with water every

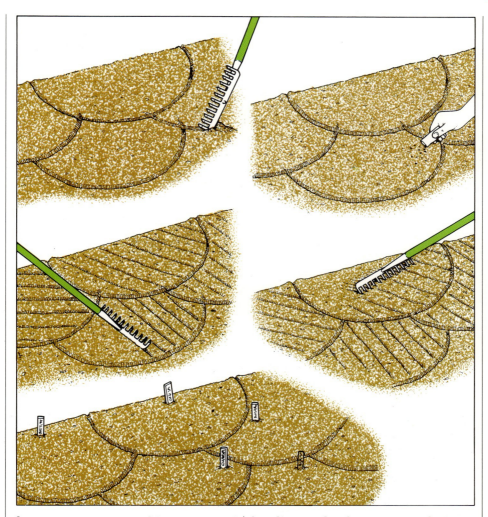

day soon removes this source of trouble since thrips thrive in hot, dry conditions. Alternatively spray with an insecticide such as 'Sybol' or 'Picket'.

Sowing hardy annuals The seed of hardy annuals such as calendulas, godetias and love-in-a-mist are sown in the open ground on the site where they are to bloom.

There is a different 'feeling' about the two sorts of annuals. Half-hardies tend to have more substance and staying power in the face of summer rain and gales. Hardy annuals are the most beautiful but usually more ephemeral. Coming as they often do from seed sown haphazardly by the plants themselves, they are also more 'cottagey' and informal. The secret of successful gardening with them is to recognize these characteristics and take particular care to find a fitting situation for them in your garden.

When and where to sow Sow seed of hardy annuals from March onwards. Avoid damp, windy days when the soil is cold; under these conditions, seed gets off to a poor start and may easily rot if the ground remains very cold. Hardy annuals look most effective if sown in half-moon drifts or drills near the front of a sunny border. As a rough guide to the correct sowing time, look for any sign of summer weeds coming up in the garden. When they begin to appear, it is time to sow.

Hardy annuals like a well-drained site. Being natives of California and other warm climes, they need plenty of light and long spells of sunshine. Never sow them in dark places or in the shade of trees or the house.

Having decided where you intend to sow seed, as soon as the weather improves, prepare the ground. Rake away rough stones and weeds, then work the surface to a fine tilth. If the ground is too sandy, add compost, peat or 'Forest Bark' Ground and Composted Bark, mixing this in with the surface soil to hold the moisture and help your plants to grow.

Sow as thinly as you can, marking out the drills with the tip of your seed dibber or trowel. Cover the seed with soil and water the ground liberally. Label the areas planted to prevent the accidental hoeing away of seedlings, and thread cotton from sticks over the beds to discourage birds from taking seed.

The new shoots can be attractive to slugs and snails, so keep a watch for these. Traps are now available that are harmless to birds and pets. Alternatively, use ICI Slug Pellets which contain metaldehyde.

Some thinning is always needed once the seedlings emerge. Also, keep them well watered during dry spells in April. A second thinning at the beginning of May will provide more room for the ones intended to be left to flower.

Hardy annuals usually bloom from June onwards and vary considerably in flower power. Calendulas continue in full bloom till September while annual poppies are short-lived but very beautiful. Bear these considerations in mind when deciding where to plant out.

Overwintering Some hardy annuals can be sown in September for flowering the next year. Again, thin out twice. Larkspur, clarkia,

BELOW LEFT Gilia, echium, agrostemma, alyssum, tropaeolum and calendula in a garden that more than repays the preparation work necessary.

RIGHT Slender stems of the hardy annual, *Clarkia pulchella* 'Filigree', are massed with flowers from July to September.

BELOW RIGHT Dainty *Viola × wittrockiana* is sown in July or August, either in a damp shaded spot, or in a cold frame.

calendula and candytuft all perform happily under this sort of treatment.

Hardy biennials such as wallflowers and forget-me-nots come from seed sown in the summer and transferred to flowering positions in the early autumn. They all bloom in April and May, spanning the winter between their two big phases of growth. Many garden-centres and nurserymen offer wallflower plants in the autumn for immediate planting outdoors.

Most hardy perennials come from seed. Obviously, this is cheaper than buying in mature plants and dividing them the following year. The snags are that they do not always come completely true from seed, either in colour or size. Also, you will usually have to wait two years or at least 18 months before plants start to flower. But in a large new garden, it is cheaper to have a few perennials coming up from seed. Violas and pansies are particularly useful perennials since they will produce flowers the same summer as sown, if they are given the half-hardy treatment.

FLOWERS IN CONTAINERS

There is nothing restrictive in this sort of gardening, and both annuals and bedding plants make ideal subjects for containers. Think of them as vehicles of 'moveable colour' that can be placed in either shady or bright sunshine conditions according to the needs of the plants. Also, most plants grown outdoors can be taken into a conservatory or sun-room for a limited period if you wish.

A sunny patio is an ideal site for container plants, and if you find that any of your chosen plants clash when in bloom, you can simply rearrange the pots rather than have to uproot or live with the colour scheme.

A large selection of lightweight pots and containers in plastic and glass fibre is now available. Not only are these much easier to move than the old-style stone urns, but they have proved to be ideal for displaying colourful flowering annuals and perennials.

The advent of these lightweight containers has revolutionized container gardening. Now, simply by moving a pot, you can create a different, even better, climate for your plants.

Containers planted with shade-loving plants are very effective in small back-garden patios of town-houses. Heathers and bulbs provide winter colour, and for the rest of the year annual and perennial flowers can take over.

For a corner in a shady spring garden, there is nothing to beat wallflowers. Blooming at 30cm (12in), they are unlikely to suffer from wind damage. Plant them round a flame-shaped *Juniperus communis* 'Compressa' (Noah's Ark Juniper) in a wide container.

Forget-me-nots in a range of white, pink and royal blue as well as the old-fashioned sky-blue, are ideal

RIGHT Added impact for a window-box display is here achieved by securing a second box to a ledge below the sill. An adventurous scheme of pink and red pelargoniums with deep violet blue petunias is offset to perfection by the crisp white walls.

BELOW Statuary makes a charming complement to an array of containers great and small.

companions for wallflowers and tulips planted in pots. Astilbes, F_1 pansies and primulas are also good container plants.

And why not rescue your favourite hosta from a damp, dark corner and bring it into a lighter position as a container-plant? Sited by a pool, this could look particularly charming.

Summer plantings

Summertime brings even more scope for container plantings. Petunias, lobelia, sweet alyssum, French and African marigolds, ageratum, antirrhinums and pelargoniums are all very floriferous and enjoy summer sunshine.

Window-boxes can be enjoyed close up, from inside the house as well as outdoors. As such, they deserve your best attentions in selecting what to grow. The range of petunias is wide as there are large frilly forms as well as smaller-flowered varieties. For such a prime position I like to see any of the Dwarf Resisto forms. These are completely rain-resistant and give a regular flower performance till cut down by late October frosts. 'Iced Blue' is spectacular, its violet flowers boldly marked with white stars, and 'Resisto Rose' is dramatic in any scheme centred on pink. Four petunias, evenly spaced, should amply fill out a window-box as the season advances.

Hanging baskets should be planted with a romantic vision in mind. Consider a pendant fuchsia for your central plant, or a pastel coloured pelargonium. My own favourite pelargoniums are the delicately tinted 'Apple Blossom Orbit' and 'Hollywood' (again pink).

If you prefer a bright red, opt for the bold 'Sundance'. The F_1 pelargoniums are sown in heat in early January and brought on till the end of May when they can be put outdoors to bloom.

The easiest and most reliable half-hardy annual in-fillers for baskets, window-boxes and indeed most containers, are the trailing lobelia 'Blue Cascade', prolifically flowering white alyssum and ageratum.

Larger containers As a plant-container, a cut-down water butt or an old wooden garden-barrow are more ambitious. First, examine them critically. Do they look ornamental? Could they do with a coat of preservative paint? Are they worthy of your care and attention in planting?

Once you've dealt with such priorities you will want to station your container in the most sunny part of the garden, before the actual planting begins.

For an effective central point, try a bold group of African marigolds, such as the F_1 hybrid 'Inca Gold' that blooms at around 30cm (12in). It does very well in a sunny, even hot summer and continues well into

Hanging baskets provide the ideal home for many small trailing plants. Position taller plants at the centre and trailers at the sides, including a few patches of white to crisp up the colours. Remember to water very regularly in dry spells, even if it does mean getting out a stepladder! Your efforts will be well rewarded.

LEFT You may not have an old wheelbarrow that can be pressed into service but other once practical items such as a small tin bath, watering can or large old ceramic casserole make good plant containers. Remember to provide drainage holes if these do not already exist.

BELOW An urn of pelargoniums and silvery *Helichrysum petiolatum*, here gracing a secluded patio, would equally well form a centrepiece for a small island bed in a lawn.

October. A splendid alternative would be 'Solar Orange' – up to 38cm (15in) tall.

Bedding begonias are a delight in every sort of container. Give them the semi-shade they like and they will delight you for the whole summer. The new Non Stop varieties are possibly the best forms to try. They come in a range of orange, bright red, pink, apricot and yellow flowers.

It is a proved truism that the bigger the container, the better. It holds a lot more plants than an ordinary pot and provides a bigger splash of colour in the garden. If large enough, containers can become the main attraction in any garden. As such, they deserve planting with due care to flower colour, height and span. So plan well before you plant and then nurture these miniature gardens as outlined overleaf. Your reward will be a colourful spring and summer display.

RIGHT Another bold scheme of pink fuchsias, bright scarlet pelargoniums and violet-blue lobelia. Planted in a long, low box, they give the illusion of a small bed against the brick wall.

BELOW A hanging basket spilling over with colour draws attention to the porch architecture as well as welcoming visitors.

Watering is a matter of discretion, according to the weather. During wet spells the plants can look after themselves. Otherwise, water them twice a week, with more regular watering if hotter weather ever does arrive.

Feeding is essential if you want a first-rate, long-lasting crop of blooms. No feeding will be necessary for the first six weeks but thereafter, a dose of a good general fertilizer such as growmore works out as just right. Always apply this strictly according to the manufacturer's instructions; never add more 'for good measure'.

As the season advances, remove spent flower-heads and dead leaves that can cause disease and decay. This is particularly important with petunias and African marigolds. Also, with all container-plants, this dead-heading greatly prolongs the flowering season.

General maintenance Whether you buy in from a garden-centre or grow them from seed, maintenance of all spring and summer container plants is the same.

First, steel yourself to nip off the first flower-buds to give the plants additional energy to produce side-shoots. This will ensure bushy plants and consequently many more flower-buds later.

Another important point to remember is that all containers have a hot and a cold side. Accordingly, plant-roots can easily be chilled or over-heated. This can mean occasionally turning your most sunny or shaded containers to even up plant-growth and increase flower-power. This potential problem can be partly avoided by lining larger containers and south-facing window-boxes with bubble plastic to act as insulation and help to even up temperatures. But don't block off the drainage holes.

Weight is always important when thinking of containers, at least of those you will need to move from time to time. It is a good idea therefore, to bottom-fill deep ones with pieces of broken polystyrene before in-filling with compost. This makes them much easier to move.

Another way of reducing weight is to use a lightweight growing medium. For this purpose, I choose a peat-based soilless compost such as 'Kericompost'. It is ideal for containers: it permits good drainage and yet holds plenty of moisture.

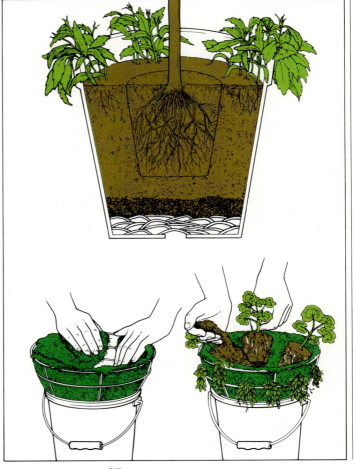

RIGHT, ABOVE If planting in a deep container, it is important to allow a really generous layer of crocks to safeguard against poor drainage. Lay the crocks with their curved surface uppermost as shown.

RIGHT When planting up a hanging basket, stand the container in the top of a small bucket. This will steady the pot and bring it up to a good working height. Slightly tilt the plants at the outer edge to encourage them to trail as intended.

AN A TO Z OF FAVOURITE PLANTS

It would be impossible to describe here all of the flowering plants that come from seed or can be bought at garden-centres to grace the spring and summer garden. The following list is therefore made up of my own favourites. It can be followed as it stands, or used as a 'starter' list of suggestions from which you can develop your own ideas.

Althaea rosea H.B.

(Hollyhock) Sown outdoors in June, hollyhocks will come into flower 11 months later. The single yellow, crimson and pink forms have come down to us from 19th-century cottage gardens. Modern doubles show a great improvement in colouring and form and are just as vigorous. The characteristically papery and rounded blooms are close-packed up the flowering stems. Plants grow to 1.8m (6ft) and should be firmly staked. Seed-produced plants are more rust-resistant than those propagated by division.

Amaranthus caudatus H.A.

(Love-lies-bleeding) This spectacular annual has long tassel-flowers that appear in July and last till the first frosts. The popular name applies to the crimson-flowered form; there is also a lime-green form (*A. viridis*). Both start to bloom at around 90cm (3ft) so they make excellent background plants for a display of annuals. Or grow them in a large circular container. For this, plants should be of one colour only – never both as the effect is nothing like so good.

Amaranthus caudatus

Dusky pink *Althaea rosea*

Anchusa capensis H.A.

(Alkanet) This showy annual is easily grown from seed and is in bloom only 14 weeks after a March sowing. The star-shaped flowers, of an unusually intense blue, are produced on hummocky plants only 23cm (9in) high. Anchusas like an open, sunny and well-drained situation. They look best when planted in drifts weaving around low-growing perennials like *Stachys lanata*. The variety 'Blue Angel' cannot be bettered.

Antirrhinum H.H.A.

(Snapdragon) This is really a perennial that is more manageable in borders if sown from seed and given half-hardy treatment. It is a sun-lover and tolerates almost any soil. Catalogues list a huge number of varieties: tall 60cm (24in), medium 45cm (18in) and dwarf forms 20cm (8in). Nip off fading spikes to encourage new flower stems. Tall varieties may need staking. It is also possible to sow all antirrhinums in September and grow on as biennials.

Anchusa capensis 'Blue Angel'

Aquilegia H.H.A.

(Columbine) This dainty plant with ferny foliage is unexpectedly vigorous, with large 'spurs' and flowers in a riot of bi-colour pastel variations. Unfortunately, it suffers from greenfly and should be sprayed as soon as buds start to form.

Bellis perennis H.B.

(Button daisy) Sow this charming little plant in September, for flowering the following May. Although directly related to the lawn daisy, this cultivated form is several times larger, and comes usually as fully double and in a wide range of pink, rose and crimson colours. When in bloom it is not more than 12cm (5in) which makes it the perfect edging plant in a May display. The best forms are 'Rose Carpet' and 'Monstrosa Rose'. Plant them in either sun or semi-shade.

Antirrhinum 'Liberty Bells'

Aquilegia vulgaris hybrids

Bellis perennis 'Rose Carpet'

Calceolaria rugosa H.H.A.

(Outdoor calceolaria) Also known as the Slipper Flower, this plant brings a golden touch to any summer garden. The bright, sunshine yellow flowers are produced prolifically on low-growing, neat plants that seldom grow higher than 24cm (9in). Look particularly for 'Midas' and 'Sunshine'. Both are F_1 hybrids which guarantee an even performance and a continuous splash of flower-colour. They should not be confused with the greenhouse calceolarias that do well when grown as indoor pot-plants.

Calendula officinalis H.A.

(Pot marigold) Lemon, orange and apricot forms of this popular plant are available in separate colours and in balanced mixtures. For something different, try 'Green Crown', in which the main attraction is the large, green centre. The petals are burnt orange. Calendulas bloom in June from an April sowing outdoors. They tend to be prey to black fly in the late summer, when they should be taken up and destroyed.

Campanula media H.B.

(Canterbury bells) Look for this plant both under its popular name and under the Campanula section in catalogues. There are some splendid mixtures, ranging through pure white to rosy pink and deep mauve. The variety 'Bells of Holland' is another good form but without 'saucers'. Canterbury Bells associate well with aquilegias.

Aptly named *Calceolaria* F_1 hybrid 'Sunshine'

Celosia H.H.A.

A lover of humid, hot summers, this plant comes in two forms. First, *C. cristata*, a variety with red, yellow, purple and crimson flowers that resemble coxcombs. Look out for the form 'Jewel Box'; best as a pot-plant, as it prefers a warmer temperature than most English summers provide. Much easier and lending themselves to bedding uses, are the 'plumosa' varieties. Dwarf 'Fairy Fountains' (a good mixture) and 'Apricot Brandy' are both splendid.

Celosia cristata 'Jewel Box'

Centaurea cyanus H.A.

(Cornflower) The romantic image of the cornfield aglow with blue cornflowers still induces us to grow this lovely plant in our gardens. In fact, all forms are far superior in size and colouring to their wild cousins and come in mixtures of pink, blue, cerise and white. 'Frosty' is an interesting novelty, with each petal tipped silver-white. As a bright blue double, 'Diadem' fulfils the old romantic image but with more substance in the flower and stronger stems. Most modern cornflowers bloom at around 35cm (14in).

Centaurea cyanus 'Blue Diadem', a large double variety

Cheiranthus cheiri H.B.

(Wallflowers) Wallflowers are the best possible basis of a springtime display. Sow direct into the ground in May, thinning out as the summer advances. Wallflowers are ideal both for springtime bedding or for cutting to take indoors. Most forms are delicately fragrant. 'Cloth of Gold', 'Primrose Monarch' and 'Eastern Queen' are good, colourful forms. Several excellent mixtures are also available. Most bloom at around 38cm (15in), though the diminutive 'Tom Thumb' hardly tops 23cm (9in).

Chrysanthemum carinatum and *C. coronarium* H.A.

(Annual chrysanthemum) Of these, the most eye-catching is *C. carinatum* with its yellow and orange daisy-flowers. Some flowers are heavily zoned with red. Look out for 'Flame Shades' that blooms at 45cm (18in) and is invaluable as a border plant and for container work. The 'Golden Gem' form of *C. coronarium* has sufficient merit to be used with lemon African marigolds. Of slighter habit, *C. paludosum* is a small but effective filler, bearing neat daisy flowers from late June.

Chrysanthemum parthenium 'Aureum' H.P.

(Golden feverfew) It is difficult to decide in which category to place golden feverfew. Well-grown plants and seedlings winter as perennials yet it comes from seed and blooms the same year in the manner of an annual. Its main characteristic is its readiness to adapt to any garden situation. Small white daisy flowers are borne most picturesquely among golden foliage, all through the summer. This plant seeds down everywhere if allowed.

Daisy flowers of *Chrysanthemum parthenium* (Feverfew)

Popular, silver-leaved *Cineraria maritima* 'Cirrhus'

Cineraria maritima H.H.A.

(Senecio maritima) This is perhaps the most popular dot plant, with its woolly-leaved, ferny foliage. And its startling grey-white is a perfect foil for pastel-coloured petunias and annual phlox. Plant out in mid-May, singly or in groups of three. These 45cm (18in) tall plants will stand some winter frost and can be left out. Excellent forms are 'Silver Dust' and an elegant newcomer called 'Cirrhus', which has a denser leaf effect.

Clarkia H.A.

This is one of the most colourful hardy annuals. 'Filigree' is a single flowered, dainty form with rose, lilac and white flowers that never exceed 30cm (1ft). It makes an ideal edging plant to a sunny border. Double forms like 'Royal Bouquet' – again in a wide colour range – present themselves as dwarf hollyhocks rising on 20cm (8in) high stems. Support the growing stems unobtrusively with twigs. Double clarkia flowers are ideal for cut blooms. Strip the leaves before placing the stems in water.

Cosmos 'Psyche'

Cosmos H.H.A.

This long popular half-hardy annual is valuable as one of the few really tall annuals, blooming at around 1m (40in), which makes it equally useful in the annual border, or as a dainty companion plant along with perennial phlox in a mixed border. Mature plants produce masses of single mauve and pink flowers, which are set off by dense ferny foliage. Look out for the forms 'Gloria', 'Psyche Mixed', 'Diablo' and 'Bright Lights'.

Massed heads of popular *Delphinium* 'Tessa'

Delphinium H.P.

These stately perennials come true from seed the first summer after a springtime sowing. Catalogues list over a dozen forms, some of the shorter varieties blooming at around 75cm (30in). The latter are the best buy for a small garden. Look out for 'Dwarf Blue Fountain' and 'Connecticut Yankee', both in a mixture of blue, purple, lavender and single pink blooms. They can be increased by division after the first year. Protect from slugs.

Dianthus heddewigii 'Baby Doll'

Dianthus barbatus H.B.

(Sweet William) Sweet William should be sown in the autumn, to bloom the following May. The range of colours has greatly improved with pink, velvety-red and powder-pink bi-colours now available. Plants are more interesting and reliably hardy in poor spring weather. 'Summer Beauty' is a splendid mixture and an annual Sweet William called 'Roundabout' is also now available. This germinates in the open ground, blooms from July onwards, and comes in all the characteristic Sweet William colours.

Dianthus chinensis and *D. heddewigii* H.H.A.

(Annual pinks) These plants should not be confused with rockery dianthus or carnations. They are a distinct race of pinks that come from seed and bloom the same summer. Like all members of the dianthus family, they like a sunny situation and good drainage. Many F_1-hybrids have been raised. Notable among them are 'Magic Charms', with pink and crimson colours, 'Baby Doll' (a splendid mixture), and 'Queen of Hearts' (scarlet). All bloom at about 20cm (8in) on low bushy plants.

Fuchsia H.P.

Standard forms of fuchsia make excellent dot plants among low, mass summer bedding. In particular, a symmetrical scheme using fibrous begonias with white alyssum can be greatly enhanced by a centrally placed pendant standard fuchsia. Bring out your fuchsia from the greenhouse in late May and plant it out, still in its pot. Good forms are 'Tennessee Waltz', 'Swingtime' and 'Citation'. Lift carefully in October and overwinter in the greenhouse.

Fuchsia 'Tennessee Waltz'

Gazania 'Colorama Mixed'

Gazania H.H.A.

This perennial is best grown as a half-hardy annual. Start it off indoors and plant in the garden in May. All gazania are dramatically showy, with contrasting stripes and zones of colour. Colours are predominantly yellow and orange. Low, sprawly plants, they look their best planted at the border's edge, where their intricate colouring can be appreciated; space out at 30cm (1ft) apart. These plants are excellent in seaside gardens. Where possible, plant in light sandy soil.

Godetia H.A.

This plant comes readily from seed sown the autumn prior to summer flowering. The large, fluted flowers have a delicate, papery look that belies the reliable hardiness of this plant. Look out for the fully double Azalea-flowered Mixed, in a colour range from powder pink through to rich crimson. Separate colours are now available in 'Sybil Sherwood', 'Salmon Princess' and 'Crimson Glow'. All of these lovely varieties bloom at around 30cm (1ft).

Helianthus annuus

Gypsophila elegans H.A.

A very easy hardy annual that comes readily from seed. This wiry plant has fine grey leaves and a lovely, cloudy mass of white, single flowers. Put it as a companion-plant to petunias, annual phlox or lavatera to complement its rather ephemeral beauty. Flowers bloom in July at around 35cm (14in) and last well into the autumn.

Helianthus annuus H.A.

(Sunflower) Sunflowers come from seed sown direct into the ground in March, and when they reach 1.5m (5ft) they start to bloom. These magnificent flowers have huge brown centres and yellow ray-petals. Side-shoots are usually produced as well as more and more flowers, which tend to be smaller than the first central bloom. A good 'single' variety is 'Russian Giant'. 'Summer Sunshine' and 'Sunburst' come in a range of crimson, yellow and red, blooming at around 1.2m (4ft), a more manageable height than 'Russian Giant' for most gardens.

Helichrysum bracteatum H.H.A.

(Strawflower) The flowers are crisp to the touch at all stages of growth, and as 'drieds' they are very useful in winter flower arrangements. The stems, however, do not dry well so it is best to wire the flower-heads before use. In the garden, this attractive annual blooms at 90cm (3ft). Dwarfer forms, flowering at 45cm (18in) are available and likely to ride a summer storm better.

Iberis umbellata H.A.

(Candytuft) This does well in almost any situation, but is at its best in sunny weather. Dwarf 'Fairy Mixed', an old favourite, still stands out as giving an excellent blend of white, pink, rose and mauve flowers. Use it in drifts at the front of a border or for a more temporary but showy display on the rock-garden. Good alternative plants are candytuft 'Pink Queen' and 'Red Flash'.

Impatiens F$_1$ hybrid, mixed

Lathyrus odoratus (sweet peas)

Impatiens sultanii H.H.A.

(Busy Lizzie) Originally grown as a house-plant, Busy Lizzie has now moved outdoors to provide summer colour in flower-beds, window-boxes and hanging-baskets. Modern F_1 hybrid forms provide an abundance of colour, ranging from bright scarlet to white, pink and rose. Plants bloom at around 6cm (3in) and are amazingly resilient to very hot or wet summer weather. For excellent results, try 'Futura'.

Kochia scoparia H.H.A.

(Burning bush) Although classified as hardy, this is best given the half hardy treatment indoors. This will get youngsters off to a good start when they are planted out as dot plants in May. This 60cm (2ft) tall, feathery cypress stands out prominently against a flat mass of low bedding. Or plant three together for more effective emphasis. Come September, the plants take on a reddish hue that explains the popular name of burning bush.

Lathyrus odoratus H.A.

(Sweet peas) These colourful climbers can be reared either as half-hardy annuals, or autumn-sown as recommended for some hardy annuals. Modern sweet peas are all Spencer varieties and come in a rainbow-range of shades; new forms appear every year. All need a fence, trellis or tripod to clamber up; tie in young shoots as they grow, to encourage the upward climb. The delicate blooms make excellent cut flowers.

Lavatera trimestris H.A.

(Mallow) A wonderful hardy annual, both good looking and easy to grow, this is a plant of sufficient substance to be put alongside perennials such as anaphalis or herbaceous phlox. Blooming at 1.2m (4ft), it provides an ideal background to any colour scheme. Excellent forms are 'Silver Cup' (pink), and the white 'Mont Blanc'. Even better results can be obtained from a March sowing indoors, with the plants put out to flower from the end of May.

Lavatera trimestris 'Silver Cup'

Lobelia H.H.A.

This annual has for a long time held its place as the most useful of blue summer flowers. The light-coloured 'Cambridge Blue' flowers are my favourite for edging both golden and orange schemes, and will also effectively complement pink flowers. White lobelia, particularly in the form 'White Lady', is currently popular for hanging-baskets. It is small enough to provide a clean and bright edging to large containers. 'Blue Cascade', a trailing form, also looks splendid. 'Colour Cascade' provides a wide range of blue, white and rosy-pink forms.

Lobularia maritima H.A.

(Sweet alyssum) A hardy annual that, contrariwise, always does better if reared from seed in the greenhouse and brought on as a half-hardy annual. Germination is more even and plants are sturdier when the time comes to put them out in mid-May. This low, ground-hugging plant bears a mound of pure white, slightly scented flowers and is ideal on the rock-garden, or in a bedding scheme as a cool break to deep cerises and hot oranges. It is also an excellent choice for hanging-baskets.

Lupinus polyphyllus H.P.

(Lupin) A showy perennial that can be flowered from seed during its first summer. Always chip seed before sowing as it is very hard. 'Russell Mixed' and 'Band of Nobles' produce a range of blues, pinks, maroon and yellows. Bi-coloured beauties often occur and can be kept for growing on the following summer. Lupins strongly dislike manure and fail miserably in over-rich ground. Where plants are to be kept, cut off the flower spikes without delay as soon as they start seeding.

Mixed *Lupinus polyphyllus*

Matthiola incana H.B.

(Stocks) Of these spring-flowering biennials, Brompton Stocks are perhaps the most useful. These highly perfumed plants come in a wide range of pink, mauve, cream and crimson flowers, and associate well with wallflowers and bright blue forget-me-nots. An ideal biennial for May-time containers and most effective when partnered by pink tulips. Seed is sown in July of the previous year. Remove any dark green seedlings as these always produce single flowers; the rest will come fully double.

Mesembryanthemum criniflorum H.H.A.

(Livingstone daisy) This makes a ground-hugging plant, just 8cm (3in) high. Mature plants are dotted with luminous daisy-flowers that complement the silvery stickiness of the tubular, succulent foliage. Seed Mixtures include salmon, apricot, carmine and bright orange flowers. Use them among pebbles and stones in a sunny part of the garden. Livingstone daisies do well in poor, dry soil but dead-heading is essential to ensure a constant succession of bloom.

Mimulus variegatus 'Calypso'

Mimulus H.H.A.

(Monkey flower) This is a short-lived perennial best treated as a half-hardy annual and sown in heat indoors for planting outside in May. Flowering starts in late June and continues till October. The feature of the monkey flower is its hot copper flowers spotted with yellow. New hybrid F_1 forms present some interesting variants, such as orange, yellow and russet flowers. 'Calypso' and 'Queen's Prize' are excellent forms. Mimulus plants revel in damp, shady situations.

Myosotis alpestris H.B.

(Forget-me-not) This popular spring-flowering plant makes a pretty edging for a display of wallflowers. For preference, forget-me-nots like a moist, not over-sunny situation. This means that normal springtime temperatures suit them to perfection. In addition to the popular 'Ultramarine' with its bright colouring, rosy-carmine, royal blue and white forms are available. All come true from seed and should be autumn-sown.

Nemesia H.H.A.

This easy-to-grow plant flowers readily outdoors till the first frosts. All mixtures are very colourful, with orange, blue, purple and red flowers. There is also a delightful single blue form called 'Blue Gem'. All nemesias love the sun and will tolerate almost any type of soil. Keep these lovely plants well-watered in hot, dry spells. Cut back spent blooms to induce more flowers.

Pansies and Violas H.P.

Botanically, these are both the same, so you can search through catalogues under both names to find the colours you want. Although perennials, these plants are usually grown from seed as half-hardy annuals. They flower by the end of May, and catalogues list orange, yellow, blue, cream and some interesting bi-colours. A special one for me has always been *Viola cornuta* 'Alba', invaluable for its brilliant white flowers. It does well in shade and never seems to fall prey to 'pansy wilt'.

Viola 'Azure Blue'

Papaver nudicaule 'San Remo'

Papaver nudicaule H.B.

(Iceland poppy) This hardy biennial can be sown in September for flowering the following June. Alternatively, treat it as half-hardy, sowing seed in January to produce 45cm (18in) tall plants for bedding outdoors in May. Look out for F_1 hybrids like 'Champagne Bubbles' and 'San Remo'. Both bloom at 60cm (2ft) and carry paper-thin, pink, peach and ivory flowers. The long flowering stems make a striking centrepiece in indoor arrangements.

Pelargonium zonale H.H.A.

(Geranium) Since the introduction of F_1 hybrid pelargoniums, a vast new range of plants has become available, all hardy enough to be used outdoors. They will produce plenty of bloom on plants grown from seed sown in January. Look out for 'Startel Salmon', 'Ringo Dolly' and the colourful red called 'Vibrant'. They like a sunny summer to do really well. Take cuttings to propagate those forms that you have particularly liked.

Petunia H.H.A.

Most petunias offered nowadays are F_1 hybrids, of uniform habit and flowering at exactly the same time. This makes them admirable for mass planting in containers and window-boxes. Try the frilly double called 'Circus', a white and rosy-pink picotee. Or, for sheer stamina, nothing beats 'Resisto Rose'; this medium-flowered variety stands up amazingly well to summer rain. Catalogues list several dozen forms of petunias.

Phlox drummondii H.H.A.

(Annual phlox) Originally a straggly plant, this has now been refined down to produce neat foliage and blooms that are velvety to the touch and come in a scarlet, rosy-pink, primrose and white. Phlox Mixtures such as 'Carnival' and 'Dwarf Mixed' are ideal near the front of a narrow border. They also blend very well with a scheme based on pink. 'Twinkling Stars' is a pretty novelty, the flowers being distinctly pointed.

Petunia 'Circus'

Primula denticulata H.P.

(Drumstick primula) This is one of the loveliest of spring-flowering primulas. It is also one of the easiest to grow. Sow seed in July for flowers the following April. These are borne in a perfectly round terminal cluster on short, strong stems. Colours range from pure white through pinky mauve to a rich purple. This plant is often seen in a waterside situation or in a shady, damp corner among hostas and ferns.

Reseda odorata H.A.

(Mignonette) An old-fashioned herb that has retained its place in modern gardens for its distinctive fragrance, this hardy annual likes sunshine and should be sown outdoors where intended to flower. Mignonette flowers are lime green, tinged dark red and are borne in tight clusters on stems 30cm (1ft) high. They first appear in June and stay in good order till well into September. Favourite varieties are 'Suttons Giant' and 'Machet'.

Primula denticulata

Ricinus communis H.H.A.

(Castor oil plant) This plant is of prime importance as a large, 1.2m (4ft) tall dot plant with bronze purple foliage. It is the perfect foil for the hot colours of African marigolds, though it needs a hot summer to do really well and is not advised for northern gardens. The red flowers and spiky seeds are interesting but nothing like so eye-catching as the foliage. Look out for *Ricinus* 'Gibbsonii' 1.2m (4ft) and the dwarf form 'Mizumi' 90cm (3ft).

Rudbeckia H.H.A.

(Cone flower) The striking yellow and bronze cone-flowers are borne freely from July onwards. 'Gloriosa Daisy Mixed' is an excellent form with gold, orange and mahogany flowers, while the gold-flowered 'Marmalade' is one of the finest annuals ever to have been raised. The newer introduction called 'Goldilocks' is a double form of great substance. For best result, sow the seed in March. In wet summers, plants can make a lot of green growth and should be unobtrusively supported with slender canes.

Phlox drummondii 'Carnival'

Salvia argentea H.P.

Sown from seed under heat in March, this distinguished 'silver' will provide a lustrous cluster of velvety leaves during its first summer. It winters reasonably well in all but the coldest areas and emerges as quite a different plant in its second summer, when strong stems appear and the plant produces spikes of grey-blue flowers at around 90cm (3ft). For low silver foliage effects, site them right at the front of a sunny border.

Stachys lanata or *olympica* H.P.

(Lamb's ears) Although usually described as a 'silver' in catalogues, this plant is more velvety than silver. As its popular name suggests, the leaves are long and furry. The plant's habit is to spread outwards rather than vertically, hence its use in sunny areas where ground cover is wanted. Flowers are magenta and borne in furry racemes well above the foliage. Plants germinate readily from seed and will come into bloom the following summer.

Statice or Limonium H.H.A.

(Sea lavender) This plant is rightly called an 'everlasting', since its flowers are papery even at the juvenile stage and remain so all through the summer. It is often picked for 'dried' arrangements to be enjoyed indoors, and comes in wide mixtures of lemon, pink, purple and salmon. If you prefer separate colours, look for 'Purple Monarch', 'American Beauty' (pink) and 'Pacific Gold Coast' (a rich yellow). Sea Lavender is perfect for all sunny places in the garden.

Tagetes patula and *T. erecta* H.H.A.

(French and African marigolds) Catalogues list over 40 different forms of tagetes, so if you are look-

Stachys olympica

Tagetes 'Inca Gold'

ing for a wide and versatile range of lemon, gold, orange and mahogany flowers for your summer garden, look no further. There are both single and fully double forms of both African and French marigolds, all in bloom from May to the first October frosts. They are also trouble free. To get a full flowery show, all flower buds should be removed for two or three weeks after planting out.

Tripteris nyoseroides 'Gaiety'

Tropaeolum majus 'Peach Melba'

Tripteris H.A.

A spectacular member of the daisy family that comes readily from seed, with flowers of a radiant orange colour with gold centres. The foliage is fine and the whole plant sturdy but never coarse. It likes a sunny situation in rich soil and is well suited for inclusion in an orange-lemon scheme along with big African marigolds. Flowers are produced on 45cm (18in) tall plants, coming into bud in June and lasting till October, when plants are cut down by frost, if you systematically dead-head.

Tropaeolum canariense H.A.

(Canary creeper) This delicate annual climber with small yellow flowers is related to the popular nasturtium, though it bears little obvious resemblance either in flowers or foliage. Canary creeper is, as the name suggests, a splendid plant to clamber up trellises, fences and other larger plants. Sow seed where the plant is to bloom and thin out to 13cm (5in) to allow seedlings plenty of room to make their way upwards.

Tropaeolum majus H.A.

(Nasturtium) This is one of the easiest of annuals to grow from seed. The round-penny foliage is a special characteristic that has been developed in the form called 'Alaska' to come as boldly marbled and cream-striped. The flowers of this and all other nasturtiums are produced plentifully in a wide range of red, lemon, salmon and orange shades. Dwarf forms are suitable in containers, while climbers should be encouraged to clamber up trellises and fences. Look out for the glamorous 'Peach Melba' (lemon), and the Whirleybird strains in a wide range of colours. Nasturtiums do best on poor soil.

Zea 'Gracillima Variegata'

Zea 'Gigantea Quadricolor'

Verbena H.H.A.

These half-hardy annuals come in a range of carmine, scarlet, purple and cream flowers. Plants bloom in June at around 20cm (8in), each stem carrying a cluster of primrose-like flowers. Verbenas are excellent in window-boxes, hanging baskets or borders. Any well-drained soil suits but verbena does best in full sunshine. Excellent forms are the mixture 'Springtime' and the shell pink 'Delight'.

Zea H.H.A.

(Ornamental maize) This ornamental annual has a tropical appeal in its tall, gracefully arching green and white foliage. A single plant of *Z. gracillima* 'Variegata' is outstanding as a solitary dot plant at the end of a narrow border or sited centrally in massed bedding. *Z. quadricolor*, with its cream, pink and yellow striped foliage is a show stopper. All forms will attain a height of 1.2m (4ft) in a good summer.

Half-hardy *Zinnia* 'Envy'

Zinnia H.H.A.

Zinnias delight in a moist, rich soil and an airy, light situation that gets full sun. There is no more spectacular annual. Big daisy flowers of great substance are produced from July onwards. Plants attain a height of over 60cm (2ft) and stand up well to windy weather. Look out for Dahlia-flowered Mixed, in a range of yellow, rose, orange and lavender flowers. Interesting novelties are 'Envy' (green flowers) and 'Carved Ivory' an F_1 hybrid with unusual creamy white flowers.

Bulbs and massed bedding

Certain varieties of tulips and narcissi lend themselves to spring bedding. *Kaufmanniana* and *greigii* forms of tulips have low-spreading foliage and produce a mass of short-stemmed blooms that withstand April squalls. Narcissi of the sturdy Carlton family look wonderful if planted in drifts along with yellow-flowered doronicum. Blue muscari fits into any spring scheme as a bright blue edging.

For bold summer effects, plant up an entire bed of tuberous begonia of the new Non-Stop varieties. Colours are very bold: brilliant red, orange, crimson and salmon.

Ornamental annual grasses H.A. and H.H.A.

The formality of summer bedding schemes can be relieved and enhanced by an imaginative use of ornamental grasses. The general characteristics of these are fluffy seed-heads, and a pleasing lilting movement of their pliant stems. Names to look out for are *Briza* (quaking grass), *Lagurus* (hare's tail), *Agrostis* (cloud grass), and *Hordeum* (squirrel tail). You should find all of them included in seed catalogues under the general heading of Ornamental Grasses.

Tulipa greigii 'Toronto'

Hordeum jubatum

Briza maxima

INDEX AND ACKNOWLEDGEMENTS

Picture credits

Pat Brindley: 8, 11(b), 13(t), 20, 21(t), 22, 23(t), 26(t, b), 28/9, 30(b), 31(t, bl, br), 33(b), 34, 35(t), 36 (t, b), 38(t, b), 41(t), 42(t, b), 45(t, b), 46(tl), 47(t).
John Glover: 25(b), 43(t), 47(bl).
S & O Mathews: 13(b), 21(b).
Harry Smith Collection: 4/5, 7(b), 9(t, b), 10, 11(t), 12(t), 23(b), 24, 25(t), 30(t), 31(c), 32, 33(t), 35(b), 39(t, b), 40, 41(b), 43(b), 44(t, b), 46(tr, b), 47(br).
Michael Warren: 1, 7(t), 12(b).

Artwork by Simon Roulstone.